Options Trading For Beginners

A Simple And Practical Guide To Options Fundamentals And Techniques For Creating Generational Wealth Even With A Small Account

Roman F. Preciado

R
ROMAN F.
PRECIADO

Table of Contents

Chapter 4: Options Trading Tips

Introduction

Options are one of the most versatile and powerful financial instruments that can help you achieve your financial goals. Whether you want to generate income, hedge your risk, speculate on market movements, or create generational wealth, options can provide you with the flexibility and leverage you need.

But what are options and why trade them? How can you benefit from options trading and what are the risks involved? How can you set up an options trading account and what are the common terms and concepts you need to know? These are some of the questions that this book will answer for you.

In this book, you will learn the fundamentals and strategies of options trading, as well as the techniques and tips to improve your trading performance. You will also discover how to create generational wealth even with a small account, by using the power of compounding and risk management.

By the end of this book, you will have a solid foundation and a practical guide to options trading, that will help you achieve your financial objectives and create a lasting legacy for yourself and your family.

What are options and why trade them?

Options are contracts that give the buyer the right, but not the obligation, to buy or sell an underlying asset at a specified price and time. The underlying asset can be a stock, an index, a commodity, a currency, or any other tradable security.

The seller of the option, also known as the writer, has the obligation to fulfill the contract if the buyer exercises their right. The seller receives a premium, or a fee, from the buyer for taking on this obligation.

There are two types of options: **call and put**. A call option gives the buyer the right to buy the underlying asset, while a put option gives the buyer the right to sell the underlying asset. The specified price at which the buyer can buy or sell the underlying asset is called the strike price. The specified time at which the option expires is called the expiration date.

Options are traded on exchanges, such as the Chicago Board Options Exchange (CBOE), or over-the-counter (OTC), between private parties. Options are standardized contracts that have a fixed size, usually 100 shares of the underlying asset per contract.

There are many reasons why traders and investors use options, such as:

- **Income generation:** Options can be used to generate income from an existing portfolio of stocks or other assets, by selling options and collecting premiums. For example, if you own 100 shares of XYZ stock, you can sell a call option on XYZ and receive a premium. If the stock price stays below the strike price, you keep the premium and the option expires worthless. If the stock price rises above the strike price, you may have to deliver your shares to the buyer, but you still keep the premium and the profit from the stock appreciation.

- **Risk hedging:** Options can be used to hedge or reduce the risk of an existing position or a future transaction, by buying options and paying premiums. For example, if you are worried that the price of XYZ stock may drop, you can buy a put option on XYZ and pay a premium. If the stock price falls below the strike price, you can exercise your option and sell your shares at the strike price, limiting your loss. If the stock price stays above the strike price, you only lose the premium and the option expires worthless.

- **Market speculation:** Options can be used to speculate on the direction or volatility of the market, by buying or selling options and expecting a large price movement. For example, if you think that the price of XYZ stock will rise significantly, you can buy a call option on XYZ and pay a premium. If the stock price rises above the strike price, you can exercise your option and buy the shares at the strike price, making a profit. If the stock price stays below the strike price, you only lose the premium and the option expires worthless.

- **Wealth creation:** Options can be used to create generational wealth, by using the leverage and compounding effects of options trading. Leverage means that you can control a large amount of the underlying asset with a small amount of capital, by using options. Compounding means that you can reinvest your profits and grow your account exponentially, by using options. For example, if you start with $1,000 and make 10% profit per month by using options, you can grow your account to over $3 million in 10 years, by using options.

The benefits and risks of options trading

Options trading has many benefits, such as:

- **Flexibility:** Options trading allows you to customize your trades according to your risk appetite, market outlook, and financial objectives. You can choose the type, size, strike price, and expiration date of the options you trade, and create various combinations of options strategies to suit your needs.

- **Leverage:** Options trading allows you to control a large amount of the underlying asset with a small amount of capital, by using options. This means that you can magnify your returns and profits, by using options. For example, if you buy a call option on XYZ stock for $100, and the stock price rises from $50 to $60, you can make a 100% profit on your option, while the stock only increased by 20%.

- **Limited risk:** Options trading allows you to limit your risk to the amount of premium you pay or receive, by using options. This means that you can protect your downside and avoid large losses, by using options. For example, if you buy a put option on XYZ stock for $100, and the stock price drops from $50 to $40, you can limit your loss to $100, while the stock loses 20% of its value.

- **Diversification:** Options trading allows you to diversify your portfolio and trade a variety of underlying assets, such as stocks, indices, commodities, currencies, and more, by using options. This means that you can benefit from different market conditions and opportunities, by using options.

However, options trading also has some risks, such as:

- **Time decay:** Options trading involves the risk of time decay, which means that the value of an option decreases as it approaches its expiration date, due to the erosion of its extrinsic value. This means that you can lose money if the price of the underlying asset does not move in your favor, by using options. For example, if you buy a call option on XYZ stock for $100, and the stock price stays at $50 until the expiration date, you will lose your entire premium of $100, while the stock remains unchanged.

- **Volatility:** Options trading involves the risk of volatility, which means that the price of an option fluctuates due to the changes in the implied volatility of the underlying asset. Implied volatility is the market's expectation of the future volatility of the underlying asset, and it affects the option's extrinsic value. This means that you can lose money if the implied volatility of the underlying asset decreases, by using options. For example, if you buy a call option on XYZ stock for

$100, and the stock price rises from $50 to $60, but the implied volatility of the stock drops from 50% to 40%, you may not make any profit on your option, because the decrease in extrinsic value offsets the increase in intrinsic value.

- **Liquidity:** Options trading involves the risk of liquidity, which means that the availability and demand of an option may vary depending on the market conditions and the characteristics of the option. This affects the bid-ask spread, or the difference between the price at which you can buy and sell an option, and it affects the option's transaction costs. This means that you can lose money if the bid-ask spread of an option is too wide, by using options. For example, if you buy a call option on XYZ stock for $100, and the bid-ask spread is $5, you will have to pay $105 to buy the option, and you will have to sell it for $95 to break even, which reduces your profit potential.

How to set up an options trading account

To start trading options, you need to set up an options trading account with a broker that offers options trading services. There are many brokers to choose from, but you should consider the following factors when choosing a broker:

- **Fees and commissions:** Different brokers charge different fees and commissions for options trading, such as per-contract fees, exercise and assignment fees, minimum account balance fees, and more. You should compare the fees and commissions of different brokers and choose the one that offers the best value for your trading style and frequency.

- **Trading platform and tools:** Different brokers offer different trading platforms and tools for options trading, such as web-based platforms, desktop platforms, mobile apps, charts, indicators, scanners, calculators, simulators, and more. You should test the trading platform and tools of different brokers and choose the one that offers the best functionality and usability for your trading needs and preferences.

- **Customer service and support:** Different brokers offer different levels of customer service and support for options trading, such as phone, email, chat, online help, FAQs, tutorials, webinars, and more. You should evaluate the customer service and support of different brokers and choose the one that offers the best responsiveness and reliability for your trading questions and issues.

To set up an options trading account, you need to follow these steps:

- Fill out an online application form with your personal and financial information, such as your name, address, email, phone number, social security number, income, net worth, investment objectives, and risk tolerance.

- Choose the type of account you want to open, such as an individual account, a joint account, a trust account, an IRA account, or a margin account. A margin account allows you to borrow money from the broker to trade options, but it also involves higher risks and fees.

- Choose the level of options trading authorization you want to apply for, such as level 1, level 2, level 3, or level 4. Each level grants you different types of options trades that you can execute, such as covered calls, spreads, straddles, naked calls, and more. Each level also requires different levels of experience, knowledge, and capital. You should choose the level that matches your trading goals and risk tolerance.

- Review and sign the options agreement and disclosure documents, which outline the terms and conditions, risks and responsibilities, and fees and commissions of options trading. You should read and understand these documents carefully before signing them.

- Wait for the approval of your options trading account by the broker, which may take a few days or weeks, depending on the broker and the level of authorization you applied for. You may also need to provide additional documents or information, such as your tax identification number, proof of identity, or proof of income.

- Fund your options trading account with the minimum amount required by the broker, which may vary depending on the type and level of account you opened.

You can fund your account by transferring money from your bank account, by depositing a check, by wiring money, or by transferring securities from another broker.

- Start trading options by using the trading platform and tools provided by the broker, or by using your own preferred platform and tools. You should always follow your trading plan and risk management rules, and monitor your account performance and activity regularly. You should also keep learning and improving your options trading skills and strategies, by using the resources and support offered by the broker or by other sources.

The common terms and concepts in options trading

Options trading involves many terms and concepts that you need to know and understand, such as:

- **Option contract:** An option contract is an agreement between two parties, the buyer and the seller, that gives the buyer the right, but not the obligation, to buy or sell an underlying asset at a specified price and time. The seller has the obligation to fulfill the contract if the buyer exercises their right.

- **Underlying asset:** The underlying asset is the security or commodity that the option contract is based on, such as a stock, an index, a commodity, a currency, or any other tradable security.

- **Strike price:** The strike price is the specified price at which the buyer can buy or sell the underlying asset, by exercising their option. The strike price is also known as the exercise price or the strike.

- **Expiration date:** The expiration date is the specified time at which the option contract expires and becomes worthless, if not exercised. The expiration date is also known as the expiry or the expiration.

- **Option premium:** The option premium is the price that the buyer pays or the seller receives for the option contract. The option premium is also known as the option price or the premium.

- **Intrinsic value:** The intrinsic value is the amount by which an option is in-the-money, or the difference between the current price of the underlying asset and the strike price of the option. The intrinsic value is also known as the option's moneyness or the option's value.

- **Extrinsic value:** The extrinsic value is the amount by which an option's premium exceeds its intrinsic value, or the part of the option's price that reflects the time value and the implied volatility of the underlying asset. The extrinsic value is also known as the option's time value or the option's premium.

- **In-the-money (ITM):** An option is in-the-money if it has a positive intrinsic value, or if exercising the option would result in a profit. A call option is in-the-money if the current price of the underlying asset is higher than the strike price of the option. A put option is in-the-money if the current price of the underlying asset is lower than the strike price of the option.

- **Out-of-the-money (OTM):** An option is out-of-the-money if it has a zero or negative intrinsic value, or if exercising the option would result in a loss. A call option is out-of-the-money if the current price of the underlying asset is lower than the strike price of the option. A put option is out-of-the-money if the current price of the underlying asset is higher than the strike price of the option.

- **At-the-money (ATM):** An option is at-the-money if it has a zero intrinsic value, or if the current price of the underlying asset is equal to the strike price of the option.

- **Delta:** The delta is the measure of the sensitivity of an option's price to a change in the price of the underlying asset. The delta is also known as the option's hedge ratio or the option's slope. The delta of a call option ranges from 0 to 1, while the delta of a put option ranges from -1 to 0. The delta of an in-the-money option is close to 1 or -1, while the delta of an out-of-the-money option is close to 0.

- **Gamma:** The gamma is the measure of the sensitivity of an option's delta to a change in the price of the underlying asset. The gamma is also known as the option's curvature or the option's acceleration. The gamma of an option is always positive, and it is highest for at-the-money options and lowest for in-the-money and out-of-the-money options.

- **Theta:** The theta is the measure of the sensitivity of an option's price to a change in the time to expiration. The theta is also known as the option's decay or the option's time decay. The theta of an option is always negative, and it is highest for at-the-money options and lowest for in-the-money and out-of-the-money options.

- **Vega:** The vega is the measure of the sensitivity of an option's price to a change in the implied volatility of the underlying asset. The vega is also known as the option's volatility or the option's kappa. The vega of an option is always positive, and it is highest for at-the-money options and lowest for in-the-money and out-of-the-money options.

- **Rho:** The rho is the measure of the sensitivity of an option's price to a change in the interest rate. The rho is also known as the option's interest rate risk or the option's rho. The rho of a call option is positive, while the rho of a put option is negative. The rho of an option is usually small, unless the option has a long time to expiration and a high strike price.

- **Implied volatility:** The implied volatility is the market's expectation of the future volatility of the underlying asset, and it affects the option's extrinsic value. The implied volatility is also known as the option's volatility or the option's sigma. The implied volatility of an option can be derived from the option's price, using a mathematical model such as the Black-Scholes model.

- **Option chain:** The option chain is a table that displays the available options for a given underlying asset, along with their prices, volumes, open interests, and other information. The option chain is also known as the option matrix or the option grid.

- **Option quote:** The option quote is the information that shows the current bid and ask prices, and the last traded price, of an option. The option quote is also known as the option price or the option quote.

- **Bid price:** The bid price is the price that the buyer is willing to pay for an option. The bid price is also known as the buy price or the bid.

- **Ask price:** The ask price is the price that the seller is willing to accept for an option. The ask price is also known as the sell price or the ask.

- **Bid-ask spread:** The bid-ask spread is the difference between the bid price and the ask price of an option. The bid-ask spread is also known as the option's spread or the option's transaction cost.

- **Volume:** The volume is the number of option contracts that have been traded during a given period of time, such as a day, an hour, or a minute. The volume is also known as the option's volume or the option's activity.

- **Open interest:** The open interest is the number of option contracts that have been opened and not yet closed, by either being exercised, assigned, or expired. The open interest is also known as the option's open interest or the option's outstanding contracts.

- **Exercise:** The exercise is the action of the buyer to use their right to buy or sell the underlying asset, by paying or receiving the strike price. The exercise is also known as the option's exercise or the option's execution.

- **Assignment:** The assignment is the action of the seller to fulfill their obligation to deliver or receive the underlying asset, by receiving or paying the strike price. The assignment is also known as the option's assignment or the option's delivery.

- **Expiration:** The expiration is the action of the option contract to become worthless and cease to exist, if not exercised or assigned. The expiration is also known as the option's expiration or the option's termination.

- **American option:** An American option is an option that can be exercised at any time before or on the expiration date. Most stock options are American options.

- **European option:** A European option is an option that can be exercised only on the expiration date. Most index options are European options.

- **Intrinsic value:** The intrinsic value is the amount by which an option is in-the-money, or the difference between the current price of the underlying asset and the strike price of the option. The intrinsic value is also known as the option's moneyness or the option's value.

- **Extrinsic value:** The extrinsic value is the amount by which an option's premium exceeds its intrinsic value, or the part of the option's price that reflects the time value and the implied volatility of the underlying asset. The extrinsic value is also known as the option's time value or the option's premium.

By reading this book, you will gain a solid foundation and a valuable guide for your options trading journey. You will gain the knowledge and the skills that you need to trade options effectively and profitably. You will gain the confidence and the performance that you need to achieve your options trading objectives and goals. We hope that you will enjoy reading this book, and that you will find it useful and helpful for your options trading journey.

SECTION 1

Options Fundamentals

In this chapter, you will learn the basic components of an option contract, the difference between call and put options, the difference between intrinsic and extrinsic value, the factors that affect option prices, and the four types of option positions. These are the essential concepts that you need to master before you can start trading options.

The basic components of an option contract

An option contract is an agreement between two parties, the buyer and the seller, that gives the buyer the right, but not the obligation, to buy or sell an underlying asset at a specified price and time. The seller has the obligation to fulfill the contract if the buyer exercises their right.

An option contract has four basic components:

- **Underlying asset:** The underlying asset is the security or commodity that the option contract is based on, such as a stock, an index, a commodity, a currency, or any other tradable security.

- **Strike price:** The strike price is the specified price at which the buyer can buy or sell the underlying asset, by exercising their option. The strike price is also known as the exercise price or the strike.

- **Expiration date:** The expiration date is the specified time at which the option contract expires and becomes worthless, if not exercised. The expiration date is also known as the expiry or the expiration.

- **Option premium:** The option premium is the price that the buyer pays or the seller receives for the option contract. The option premium is also known as the option price or the premium.

The difference between call and put option

There are two types of options: call and put. A call option gives the buyer the right to buy the underlying asset, while a put option gives the buyer the right to sell the underlying asset. The seller of a call option has the obligation to sell the underlying asset, while the seller of a put option has the obligation to buy the underlying asset.

The buyer of a call option expects the price of the underlying asset to rise, while the buyer of a put option expects the price of the underlying asset to fall. The seller of a call option expects the price of the underlying asset to fall, while the seller of a put option expects the price of the underlying asset to rise.

The difference between intrinsic and extrinsic value

The value of an option is composed of two parts: intrinsic value and extrinsic value.

- **Intrinsic value:** The intrinsic value is the amount by which an option is in-the-money, or the difference between the current price of the underlying asset and the strike price of the option. The intrinsic value is also known as the option's moneyness or the option's value.

- **Extrinsic value:** The extrinsic value is the amount by which an option's premium exceeds its intrinsic value, or the part of the option's price that reflects the time value and the implied volatility of the underlying asset. The extrinsic value is also known as the option's time value or the option's premium.

The intrinsic value of an option depends only on the price of the underlying asset and the strike price of the option, while the extrinsic value of an option depends on other factors, such as the time to expiration, the interest rate, the dividend yield, and the implied volatility of the underlying asset.

The factors that affect option prices

The price of an option is determined by the interaction of supply and demand in the market, as well as by the factors that affect the intrinsic and extrinsic value of the option. These factors are:

- **Price of the underlying asset:** The price of the underlying asset is the most important factor that affects the option price, as it determines the intrinsic value of the option. As the price of the underlying asset increases, the intrinsic value of a call option increases, while the intrinsic value of a put option decreases. As the price of the underlying asset decreases, the intrinsic value of a call option decreases, while the intrinsic value of a put option increases.

- **Strike price:** The strike price is the second most important factor that affects the option price, as it determines the intrinsic value of the option. As the strike price increases, the intrinsic value of a call option decreases, while the intrinsic value of a put option increases. As the strike price decreases, the intrinsic value of a call option increases, while the intrinsic value of a put option decreases.

- **Time to expiration:** The time to expiration is the third most important factor that affects the option price, as it affects the extrinsic value of the option.

As the time to expiration increases, the extrinsic value of an option increases, as there is more uncertainty and more time for the price of the underlying asset to move in the favor of the option holder. As the time to expiration decreases, the extrinsic value of an option decreases, as there is less uncertainty and less time for the price of the underlying asset to move in the favor of the option holder.

- **Implied volatility:** The implied volatility is the fourth most important factor that affects the option price, as it affects the extrinsic value of the option. The implied volatility is the market's expectation of the future volatility of the underlying asset, and it reflects the uncertainty and risk of the option. As the implied volatility increases, the extrinsic value of an option increases, as there is more chance for the price of the underlying asset to move significantly in the favor of the option holder. As the implied volatility decreases, the extrinsic value of an option decreases, as there is less chance for the price of the underlying asset to move significantly in the favor of the option holder.

- **Interest rate:** The interest rate is the fifth most important factor that affects the option price, as it affects the extrinsic value of the option. The interest rate is the cost of borrowing money to buy the underlying asset, and it reflects the opportunity cost of the option. As the interest rate increases, the extrinsic value of a call option increases, while the extrinsic value of a put option decreases. As the interest rate decreases, the extrinsic value of a call option decreases, while the extrinsic value of a put option increases.

- **Dividend yield:** The dividend yield is the sixth most important factor that affects the option price, as it affects the extrinsic value of the option. The dividend yield is the amount of dividends paid by the underlying asset, and it reflects the income generated by the option. As the dividend yield increases, the extrinsic value of a call option decreases, while the extrinsic value of a put option increases. As the dividend yield decreases, the extrinsic value of a call option increases, while the extrinsic value of a put option decreases.

The four types of option positions: long call, short call, long put, short put

An option position is the combination of one or more option contracts that a trader holds, with the same underlying asset, strike price, and expiration date. There are four basic types of option positions: long call, short call, long put, and short put.

- **Long call:** A long call position is created by buying a call option. A long call position gives the trader the right to buy the underlying asset at the strike price, before or on the expiration date. A long call position profits from a rise in the price of the underlying asset, and loses from a fall in the price of the underlying asset. The maximum profit of a long call position is unlimited, while the maximum loss of a long call position is limited to the premium paid for the option.

- **Short call:** A short call position is created by selling a call option. A short call position gives the trader the obligation to sell the underlying asset at the strike price, if the option is exercised by the buyer. A short call position profits from a fall in the price of the underlying asset, and loses from a rise in the price of the underlying asset. The maximum profit of a short call position is limited to the premium received for the option, while the maximum loss of a short call position is unlimited.

- **Long put:** A long put position is created by buying a put option. A long put position gives the trader the right to sell the underlying asset at the strike price, before or on the expiration date. A long put position profits from a fall in the price of the underlying asset, and loses from a rise in the price of the underlying asset. The maximum profit of a long put position is limited to the difference between the strike price and the premium paid for the option, while the maximum loss of a long put position is limited to the premium paid for the option.

- **Short put:** A short put position is created by selling a put option. A short put position gives the trader the obligation to buy the underlying asset at the strike price, if the option is exercised by the buyer. A short put position profits from a rise in the price of the underlying asset, and loses from a fall in the price of the underlying asset. The maximum profit of a short put position is limited to the premium received for the option, while the maximum loss of a short put position is limited to the difference between the strike price and the premium received for the option.

In this chapter, we've discussed what options are, how they work, why they are useful, and how to trade them. You learned the different types of options, such as calls and puts, and the different components of an option contract, such as the underlying asset, the strike price, the expiration date, and the premium. You learned the different rights and obligations of the option buyer and the option seller, and the different outcomes of an option trade, depending on the price movement of the underlying asset. We also discussed the different factors that affect the value and the cost of an option, such as the intrinsic value, the extrinsic value, and the implied volatility.

SECTION 2

Options Strategies

In this chapter, you will learn the basic principles of options strategies, the difference between bullish, bearish, neutral, and volatile strategies, the most popular options strategies and how to use them, examples of options strategies for different market scenarios, and how to evaluate and adjust options strategies.

These are the advanced concepts that you need to master to trade options effectively and profitably.

The basic principles of options strategies

An options strategy is the combination of one or more option positions that a trader holds, with different underlying assets, strike prices, expiration dates, or types of options. An options strategy can be used to achieve various trading objectives, such as income generation, risk hedging, market speculation, or wealth creation.

There are three basic principles that guide the design and execution of options strategies:

- **Risk-reward trade-off:** The risk-reward trade-off is the balance between the potential profit and the potential loss of an options strategy. Generally, the higher the risk, the higher the reward, and vice versa. The risk-reward trade-off can be measured by the breakeven point, the maximum profit, the maximum loss, and the probability of profit of an options strategy. The breakeven point is the price of the underlying asset at which the options strategy breaks even, or makes zero profit or loss. The maximum profit is the highest possible profit that the options strategy can make, if the price of the underlying asset moves in the favor of the option holder. The maximum loss is the highest possible loss that the options strategy can incur, if the price of the underlying asset moves against the option holder. The probability of profit is the likelihood that the options strategy will make a profit, based on the current price and volatility of the underlying asset. The risk-reward trade-off can be adjusted by changing the strike price, the expiration date, or the number of contracts of the options strategy.

- **Directional bias:** The directional bias is the expectation of the future direction of the price of the underlying asset, and it determines the type and position of the options strategy. Generally, there are four types of directional bias: bullish, bearish, neutral, and volatile. A bullish bias means that the trader expects the price of the underlying asset to rise, and uses a long call or a short put position, or a combination of both, to profit from the price increase. A bearish bias means that the trader expects the price of the underlying asset to fall, and uses a long put or a short call position, or a combination of both, to profit from the price decrease. A neutral bias means that the trader expects the price of the underlying asset to stay within a narrow range, and uses a short call and a short put position, or a combination of both, to profit from the price stability. A volatile bias means that the trader expects the price of the underlying asset to fluctuate significantly, and uses a long call and a long put position, or a combination of both, to profit from the price movement. The directional bias can be adjusted by changing the type, the strike price, or the expiration date of the options strategy.

- **Volatility outlook:** The volatility outlook is the expectation of the future volatility of the price of the underlying asset, and it affects the value and the cost of the options strategy. Generally, there are two types of volatility outlook: high and low. A high volatility outlook means that the trader expects the price of the underlying asset to fluctuate significantly, and uses a long option position, or a combination of long and short option positions, to benefit from the increase in the option's extrinsic value. A low volatility outlook means that the trader expects the price of the underlying asset to fluctuate mildly, and uses a short option position, or a combination of long and short option positions, to benefit from the decrease in the option's extrinsic value. The volatility outlook can be adjusted by changing the type, the strike price, or the expiration date of the options strategy.

The difference between bullish, bearish, neutral, and volatile strategies

As mentioned above, the directional bias of an options strategy determines the type and position of the options strategy, and it reflects the trader's expectation of the future direction of the price of the underlying asset. There are four types of directional bias: bullish, bearish, neutral, and volatile.

- **Bullish strategies:** Bullish strategies are options strategies that profit from a rise in the price of the underlying asset. Bullish strategies involve buying call options or selling put options, or a combination of both. Some examples of bullish strategies are:

- **Long call:** A long call strategy is created by buying a call option. A long call strategy gives the trader the right to buy the underlying asset at the strike price, before or on the expiration date. A long call strategy profits from a rise in the price of the underlying asset, and loses from a fall in the price of the underlying asset. The maximum profit of a long call strategy is unlimited, while the maximum loss of a long call strategy is limited to the premium paid for the option.

- **Short put:** A short put strategy is created by selling a put option. A short put strategy gives the trader the obligation to buy the underlying asset at the strike price, if the option is exercised by the buyer. A short put strategy profits from a rise in the price of the underlying asset, and loses from a fall in the price of the underlying asset. The maximum profit of a short put strategy is limited to the premium received for the option, while the maximum loss of a short put strategy is limited to the difference between the strike price and the premium received for the option.

- **Bull call spread:** A bull call spread strategy is created by buying a call option with a lower strike price and selling a call option with a higher strike price, with the same expiration date. A bull call spread strategy gives the trader the right to buy the underlying asset at the lower strike price, and the obligation to sell the underlying asset at the higher strike price, if the options are exercised by the buyers. A bull call spread strategy profits from a moderate rise in the price of the underlying asset, and loses from a moderate fall in the price of the underlying asset. The maximum profit of a bull call spread strategy is limited to the difference between the strike prices minus the net premium paid for the options, while the maximum loss of a bull call spread strategy is limited to the net premium paid for the options.

- **Bull put spread:** A bull put spread strategy is created by selling a put option with a higher strike price and buying a put option with a lower strike price, with the same expiration date. A bull put spread strategy gives the trader the obligation to buy the underlying asset at the higher strike price, and the right to sell the underlying asset at the lower strike price, if the options are exercised by the buyers. A bull put spread strategy profits from a moderate rise in the price of the underlying asset, and loses from a moderate fall in the price of the underlying asset. The maximum profit of a bull put spread strategy is limited to the net premium received for the options, while the maximum loss of a bull put spread strategy is limited to the difference between the strike prices minus the net premium received for the options.

- **Bearish strategies:** Bearish strategies are options strategies that profit from a fall in the price of the underlying asset. Bearish strategies involve buying put options or selling call options, or a combination of both. Some examples of bearish strategies are:

- **Long put:** A long put strategy is created by buying a put option. A long put strategy gives the trader the right to sell the underlying asset at the strike price, before or on the expiration date. A long put strategy profits from a fall in the price of the underlying asset, and loses from a rise in the price of the underlying asset. The maximum profit of a long put strategy is limited to the difference between the strike price and the premium paid for the option, while the maximum loss of a long put strategy is limited to the premium paid for the option.

- **Short call:** A short call strategy is created by selling a call option. A short call strategy gives the trader the obligation to sell the underlying asset at the strike price, if the option is exercised by the buyer. A short call strategy profits from a fall in the price of the underlying asset, and loses from a rise in the price of the underlying asset. The maximum profit of a short call strategy is limited to the premium received for the option, while the maximum loss of a short call strategy is unlimited.

- **Bear call spread:** A bear call spread strategy is created by selling a call option with a lower strike price and buying a call option with a higher strike price, with the same expiration date. A bear call spread strategy gives the trader the obligation to sell the underlying asset at the lower strike price, and the right to buy the underlying asset at the higher strike price, if the options are exercised by the buyers. A bear call spread strategy profits from a moderate fall in the price of the underlying asset, and loses from a moderate rise in the price of the underlying asset. The maximum profit of a bear call spread strategy is limited to the net premium received for the options, while the maximum loss of a bear call spread strategy is limited to the difference between the strike prices minus the net premium received for the options.

- **Bear put spread:** A bear put spread strategy is created by buying a put option with a higher strike price and selling a put option with a lower strike price, with the same expiration date. A bear put spread strategy gives the trader the right to sell the underlying asset at the higher strike price, and the obligation to buy the underlying asset at the lower strike price, if the options are exercised by the buyers. A bear put spread strategy profits from a moderate fall in the price of the underlying asset, and loses from a moderate rise in the price of the underlying asset. The maximum profit of a bear put spread strategy is limited to the difference between the strike prices minus the net premium paid for the options, while the maximum loss of a bear put spread strategy is limited to the net premium paid for the options.

- **Neutral strategies:** Neutral strategies are options strategies that profit from a stable or slightly fluctuating price of the underlying asset. Neutral strategies involve selling call and put options, or a combination of both. Some examples of neutral strategies are:

- **Short straddle:** A short straddle strategy is created by selling a call option and a put option with the same strike price and expiration date. A short straddle strategy gives the trader the obligation to sell or buy the underlying asset at the strike price, if the options are exercised by the buyers. A short straddle strategy profits from a stable price of the underlying asset, and loses from a significant price movement of the underlying asset. The maximum profit of a short straddle strategy is limited to the net premium received for the options, while the maximum loss of a short straddle strategy is unlimited.

- **Short strangle:** A short strangle strategy is created by selling a call option and a put option with different strike prices and the same expiration date. A short strangle strategy gives the trader the obligation to sell or buy the underlying asset at the strike prices, if the options are exercised by the buyers. A short strangle strategy profits from a slightly fluctuating price of the underlying asset, and loses from a significant price movement of the underlying asset. The maximum profit of a short strangle strategy is limited to the net premium received for the options, while the maximum loss of a short strangle strategy is unlimited.

- **Iron condor:** An iron condor strategy is created by selling a call option and a put option with higher strike prices, and buying a call option and a put option with lower strike prices, with the same expiration date. An iron condor strategy gives the trader the obligation to sell or buy the underlying asset at the higher strike prices, and the right to buy or sell the underlying asset at the lower strike prices, if the options are exercised by the buyers. An iron condor strategy profits from a slightly fluctuating price of the underlying asset, and loses from a significant price movement of the underlying asset. The maximum profit of an iron condor strategy is limited to the net premium received for the options, while the maximum loss of an iron condor strategy is limited to the difference between the higher and lower strike prices minus the net premium received for the options.

- **Volatile strategies:** Volatile strategies are options strategies that profit from a significant price movement of the underlying asset, regardless of the direction. Volatile strategies involve buying call and put options, or a combination of both. Some examples of volatile strategies are:

- **Long straddle:** A long straddle strategy is created by buying a call option and a put option with the same strike price and expiration date. A long straddle strategy gives the trader the right to buy or sell the underlying asset at the strike price, before or on the expiration date. A long straddle strategy profits from a significant price movement of the underlying asset, and loses from a stable price of the underlying asset. The maximum profit of a long straddle strategy is unlimited, while the maximum loss of a long straddle strategy is limited to the net premium paid for the options.

- **Long strangle:** A long strangle strategy is created by buying a call option and a put option with different strike prices and the same expiration date. A long strangle strategy gives the trader the right to buy or sell the underlying asset at the strike prices, before or on the expiration date. A long strangle strategy profits from a significant price movement of the underlying asset, and loses from a slightly fluctuating price of the underlying asset. The maximum profit of a long strangle strategy is unlimited, while the maximum loss of a long strangle strategy is limited to the net premium paid for the options.

- **Long butterfly:** A long butterfly strategy is created by buying a call option and a put option with the same strike price, and selling two call options and two put options with higher and lower strike prices, with the same expiration date. A long butterfly strategy gives the trader the right to buy or sell the underlying asset at the same strike price, and the obligation to sell or buy the underlying asset at the higher and lower strike prices, if the options are exercised by the buyers. A long butterfly strategy profits from a significant price movement of the underlying asset, and loses from a stable or slightly fluctuating price of the underlying asset. The maximum profit of a long butterfly strategy is limited to the difference between the higher and lower strike prices minus the net premium paid for the options, while the maximum loss of a long butterfly strategy is limited to the net premium paid for the options.

The most popular options strategies and how to use them

There are many options strategies that traders and investors can use to achieve their trading objectives, such as income generation, risk hedging, market speculation, or wealth creation. However, some options strategies are more popular and widely used than others, because they are simple, effective, and versatile. Some of the most popular options strategies and how to use them are:

Covered call: A covered call strategy is created by owning the underlying asset and selling a call option on the same underlying asset. A covered call strategy is a bullish and income-generating strategy, as it allows the trader to earn the premium from selling the call option, while retaining the upside potential of the underlying asset. A covered call strategy is suitable for traders who have a moderate bullish outlook on the underlying asset, and who are willing to sell the underlying asset at the strike price, if the option is exercised by the buyer. A covered call strategy can also be used to hedge the downside risk of the underlying asset, as the premium received from selling the call option can offset some of the loss from the decline in the price of the underlying asset.

To use a covered call strategy, the trader needs to:

- Buy or own the underlying asset, such as 100 shares of XYZ stock.

- Sell a call option on the same underlying asset, with a strike price above the current price of the underlying asset, and an expiration date that matches the trader's time horizon. For example, sell a call option on XYZ stock with a strike price of $60 and an expiration date of one month.

- Collect the premium from selling the call option, and keep the underlying asset until the expiration date or until the option is exercised by the buyer.

- If the price of the underlying asset stays below the strike price, the trader keeps the premium and the underlying asset, and can repeat the process by selling another call option with a new expiration date.

- If the price of the underlying asset rises above the strike price, the trader may have to deliver the underlying asset to the buyer, at the strike price, and lose the upside potential of the underlying asset. However, the trader still keeps the premium and the profit from the appreciation of the underlying asset up to the strike price.

Protective put: A protective put strategy is created by owning the underlying asset and buying a put option on the same underlying asset. A protective put strategy is a bearish and risk-hedging strategy, as it allows the trader to protect the underlying asset from a decline in its price, by having the right to sell the underlying asset at the strike price, before or on the expiration date. A protective put strategy is suitable for traders who have a long-term bullish outlook on the underlying asset, but who are worried about a short-term bearish event or market correction. A protective put strategy can also be used to lock in the profit from the appreciation of the underlying asset, without selling the underlying asset and triggering capital gains tax.

To use a protective put strategy, the trader needs to:

- Buy or own the underlying asset, such as 100 shares of XYZ stock.

- Buy a put option on the same underlying asset, with a strike price below the current price of the underlying asset, and an expiration date that matches the trader's time horizon. For example, buy a put option on XYZ stock with a strike price of $40 and an expiration date of one month.

- Pay the premium for buying the put option, and keep the underlying asset until the expiration date or until the option is exercised by the trader.

- If the price of the underlying asset stays above the strike price, the trader keeps the underlying asset and loses the premium paid for the put option, but retains the upside potential of the underlying asset.

- If the price of the underlying asset falls below the strike price, the trader can exercise the option and sell the underlying asset at the strike price, limiting the loss from the decline in the price of the underlying asset. Alternatively, the trader can sell the put option in the market and keep the underlying asset, depending on the market conditions and the trader's preference.

Long call vertical spread: A long call vertical spread strategy is created by buying a call option with a lower strike price and selling a call option with a higher strike price, with the same expiration date. A long call vertical spread strategy is a bullish and risk-reducing strategy, as it allows the trader to profit from a moderate rise in the price of the underlying asset, while lowering the cost and the risk of buying a single call option. A long call vertical spread strategy is suitable for traders who have a directional bias on the underlying asset, but who are not confident or willing to pay a high premium for a single call option. A long call vertical spread strategy can also be used to take advantage of a low implied volatility environment, as the net premium paid for the options will be lower.

To use a long call vertical spread strategy, the trader needs to:

- Buy a call option on the underlying asset, with a strike price below the current price of the underlying asset, and an expiration date that matches the trader's time horizon. For example, buy a call option on XYZ stock with a strike price of $50 and an expiration date of one month.

- Sell a call option on the same underlying asset, with a strike price above the current price of the underlying asset, and the same expiration date. For example, sell a call option on XYZ stock with a strike price of $60 and an expiration date of one month.

- Pay the net premium for buying and selling the call options, and keep the options until the expiration date or until the options are exercised by the buyers.

- If the price of the underlying asset stays below the lower strike price, the trader loses the net premium paid for the options, as both options expire worthless.

- If the price of the underlying asset rises above the lower strike price, but stays below the higher strike price, the trader profits from the difference between the price of the underlying asset and the lower strike price, minus the net premium paid for the options, as the long call option is in-the-money and the short call option is out-of-the-money.

- If the price of the underlying asset rises above the higher strike price, the trader profits from the difference between the strike prices, minus the net premium paid for the options, as both options are in-the-money and offset each other.

Long put vertical spread: A long put vertical spread strategy is created by buying a put option with a higher strike price and selling a put option with a lower strike price, with the same expiration date. A long put vertical spread strategy is a bearish and risk-reducing strategy, as it allows the trader to profit from a moderate fall in the price of the underlying asset, while lowering the cost and the risk of buying a single put option. A long put vertical spread strategy is suitable for traders who have a directional bias on the underlying asset, but who are not confident or willing to pay a high premium for a single put option. A long put vertical spread strategy can also be used to take advantage of a low implied volatility environment, as the net premium paid for the options will be lower.

To use a long put vertical spread strategy, the trader needs to:

- Buy a put option on the underlying asset, with a strike price above the current price of the underlying asset, and an expiration date that matches the trader's time horizon. For example, buy a put option on XYZ stock with a strike price of $60 and an expiration date of one month.

- Sell a put option on the same underlying asset, with a strike price below the current price of the underlying asset, and the same expiration date. For example, sell a put option on XYZ stock with a strike price of $50 and an expiration date of one month.

- Pay the net premium for buying and selling the put options, and keep the options until the expiration date or until the options are exercised by the buyers.

- If the price of the underlying asset stays above the higher strike price, the trader loses the net premium paid for the options, as both options expire worthless.

- If the price of the underlying asset falls below the higher strike price, but stays above the lower strike price, the trader profits from the difference between the higher strike price and the price of the underlying asset, minus the net premium paid for the options, as the long put option is in-the-money and the short put option is out-of-the-money.

- If the price of the underlying asset falls below the lower strike price, the trader profits from the difference between the strike prices, minus the net premium paid for the options, as both options are in-the-money and offset each other.

Examples of options strategies for different market scenarios

Different market scenarios require different options strategies, depending on the trader's directional bias, volatility outlook, risk-reward trade-off, and trading objectives. Here are some examples of options strategies for different market scenarios:

- **Bullish market:** A bullish market is a market where the price of the underlying asset is rising or expected to rise. A trader who has a bullish bias on the underlying asset can use a bullish strategy, such as a long call, a short put, a bull call spread, or a bull put spread, to profit from the price increase. A trader who has a high volatility outlook on the underlying asset can use a volatile strategy, such as a long straddle or a long strangle, to profit from the price movement, regardless of the direction. A trader who has a low volatility outlook on the underlying asset can use a neutral strategy, such as a short straddle or a short strangle, to profit from the price stability. A trader who has a long-term bullish outlook on the underlying asset, but who is worried about a short-term bearish event or market correction, can use a risk-hedging strategy, such as a protective put, to protect the underlying asset from a decline in its price.

- **Bearish market:** A bearish market is a market where the price of the underlying asset is falling or expected to fall. A trader who has a bearish bias on the underlying asset can use a bearish strategy, such as a long put, a short call, a bear put spread, or a bear call spread, to profit from the price decrease. A trader who has a high volatility outlook on the underlying asset can use a volatile strategy, such as a long straddle or a long strangle, to profit from the price movement, regardless of the direction. A trader who has a low volatility outlook on the underlying asset can use a neutral strategy, such as a short straddle or a short strangle, to profit from the price stability. A trader who has a long-term bearish outlook on the underlying asset, but who is worried about a short-term bullish event or market rally, can use a risk-hedging strategy, such as a covered call, to generate income from the underlying asset and limit the upside risk.

- **Neutral market:** A neutral market is a market where the price of the underlying asset is stable or slightly fluctuating. A trader who has a neutral bias on the underlying asset can use a neutral strategy, such as a short straddle, a short strangle, or an iron condor, to profit from the price stability. A trader who has a high volatility outlook on the underlying asset can use a volatile strategy, such as a long straddle or a long strangle, to profit from the price movement, regardless of the direction. A trader who has a low volatility outlook on the underlying asset can use a bullish or bearish strategy, such as a long call, a long put, a bull call spread, a bull put spread, a bear call spread, or a bear put spread, to profit from a moderate price movement in the favor of the option holder.

- **Volatile market:** A volatile market is a market where the price of the underlying asset is fluctuating significantly. A trader who has a volatile bias on the underlying asset can use a volatile strategy, such as a long straddle, a long strangle, or a long butterfly, to profit from the price movement, regardless of the direction. A trader who has a high volatility outlook on the underlying asset can use a neutral strategy, such as a short straddle, a short strangle, or an iron condor, to profit from the price stability. A trader who has a low volatility outlook on the underlying asset can use a bullish or bearish strategy, such as a long call, a long put, a bull call spread, a bull put spread, a bear call spread, or a bear put spread, to profit from a moderate price movement in the favor of the option holder.

How to evaluate and adjust options strategies

Evaluating and adjusting options strategies are important skills that traders need to master, as they can help them improve their trading performance and achieve their trading objectives. Evaluating and adjusting options strategies involve the following steps:

- Monitor the market conditions and the price and volatility of the underlying asset, and compare them with the initial assumptions and expectations of the options strategy.

- Analyze the profit and loss profile and the risk-reward trade-off of the options strategy, and compare them with the desired outcomes and the trading objectives.

- Identify the factors that affect the value and the cost of the options strategy, such as the price of the underlying asset, the strike price, the time to expiration, the implied volatility, the interest rate, and the dividend yield.

- Determine the optimal time and price to exit or modify the options strategy, based on the market conditions, the profit and loss profile, the risk-reward trade-off, and the trading objectives.

- Execute the exit or modification of the options strategy, by closing, rolling, or adding to the option positions, depending on the desired outcomes and the trading objectives.

Some examples of exiting or modifying options strategies are:

- **Closing an option position:** Closing an option position is the simplest way to exit or modify an options strategy, as it involves buying or selling the option contract in the market, and terminating the option contract. Closing an option position can be done to lock in a profit, to limit a loss, to free up capital, or to avoid exercise or assignment.

- **Rolling an option position:** Rolling an option position is a way to exit or modify an options strategy, as it involves closing the current option contract and opening a new option contract with a different strike price, expiration date, or both. Rolling an option position can be done to extend the time to expiration, to adjust the strike price, to reduce the cost, or to increase the profit potential of the options strategy.

- **Adding to an option position:** Adding to an option position is a way to exit or modify an options strategy, as it involves buying or selling more option contracts with the same or different strike prices, expiration dates, or types of options. Adding to an option position can be done to increase the size, to diversify the risk, to enhance the return, or to hedge the exposure of the options strategy.

In this chapter, we discussed the different types of options strategies and how to use them. You learned the most popular options strategies and how they can help you to achieve your trading objectives, such as income generation, risk hedging, market speculation, or wealth creation. You learned how to create and analyze options strategies, using the profit and loss profile, the breakeven point, the maximum profit, the maximum loss, and the probability of profit. You also learned how to evaluate and adjust options strategies, using the option chain, the option quote, and the option symbol.

SECTION 3

Options Techniques

In this chapter, you will learn the essential tools and skills for options trading, how to read and analyze option chains and quotes, how to use technical and fundamental analysis for options trading, how to use indicators and signals for options trading, and how to manage risk and reward in options trading. These are the practical techniques that you need to apply to trade options successfully and consistently.

The essential tools and skills for options trading

Options trading requires some tools and skills that are different from or additional to those used for other types of trading, such as stock trading or forex trading. Some of the essential tools and skills for options trading are:

- **Trading platform and tools:** A trading platform is the software or application that allows you to access the options market, execute your trades, monitor your positions, and manage your account. A trading platform should provide you with the features and functions that suit your trading style and preferences, such as web-based or desktop-based, user-friendly or advanced, real-time or delayed, etc. A trading platform should also provide you with the tools that help you with your trading decisions and actions, such as charts, indicators, scanners, calculators, simulators, etc. You should choose a trading platform and tools that offer the best functionality and usability for your options trading needs and goals.

- **Broker and account:** A broker is the intermediary or agent that connects you to the options market, executes your trades, holds your funds and securities, and provides you with the services and support that you need for your options trading. A broker should be reliable, reputable, regulated, and secure, and should offer you the best value for your trading style and frequency, such as fees and commissions, margin requirements, trading hours, customer service, etc. A broker should also provide you with the account that matches your trading objectives and risk tolerance, such as an individual account, a joint account, a trust account, an IRA account, or a margin account. You should choose a broker and account that offers the best quality and suitability for your options trading needs and goals.

- **Options education and resources:** Options education and resources are the sources of information and knowledge that help you learn and improve your options trading skills and strategies. Options education and resources can be formal or informal, online or offline, free or paid, such as books, courses, webinars, podcasts, blogs, forums, newsletters, etc. You should choose the options education and resources that offer the best content and credibility for your options trading needs and goals.

- **Options trading plan and journal:** An options trading plan is a document that outlines your options trading objectives, strategies, rules, and performance indicators. An options trading plan helps you to define your trading purpose, direction, and criteria, and to follow them consistently and systematically. An options trading journal is a record of your options trading activities, results, and reflections. An options trading journal helps you to track your trading performance, analyze your trading strengths and weaknesses, and improve your trading skills and strategies. You should create and maintain an options trading plan and journal that offer the best guidance and feedback for your options trading needs and goals.

How to read and analyze option chains and quotes

An option chain is a table that displays the available options for a given underlying asset, along with their prices, volumes, open interests, and other information. An option chain is also known as the option matrix or the option grid. An option quote is the information that shows the current bid and ask prices, and the last traded price, of an option. An option quote is also known as the option price or the option quote.

To read and analyze option chains and quotes, you need to understand the following terms and concepts:

- **Option symbol:** The option symbol is the code that identifies the option contract, and it consists of the underlying asset symbol, the expiration date, the strike price, and the type of option. For example, XYZ210219C50 is the option symbol for a call option on XYZ stock, with an expiration date of February 19, 2021, and a strike price of $50.

- **Bid price:** The bid price is the price that the buyer is willing to pay for an option. The bid price is also known as the buy price or the bid.

- **Ask price:** The ask price is the price that the seller is willing to accept for an option. The ask price is also known as the sell price or the ask.

- **Bid-ask spread:** The bid-ask spread is the difference between the bid price and the ask price of an option. The bid-ask spread is also known as the option's spread or the option's transaction cost.

- **Last price:** The last price is the price at which the last trade of an option occurred. The last price is also known as the option's last price or the option's closing price.

- **Volume:** The volume is the number of option contracts that have been traded during a given period of time, such as a day, an hour, or a minute. The volume is also known as the option's volume or the option's activity.

- **Open interest:** The open interest is the number of option contracts that have been opened and not yet closed, by either being exercised, assigned, or expired. The open interest is also known as the option's open interest or the option's outstanding contracts.

- **In-the-money (ITM):** An option is in-the-money if it has a positive intrinsic value, or if exercising the option would result in a profit. A call option is in-the-money if the current price of the underlying asset is higher than the strike price of the option. A put option is in-the-money if the current price of the underlying asset is lower than the strike price of the option.

- **Out-of-the-money (OTM):** An option is out-of-the-money if it has a zero or negative intrinsic value, or if exercising the option would result in a loss. A call option is out-of-the-money if the current price of the underlying asset is lower than the strike price of the option. A put option is out-of-the-money if the current price of the underlying asset is higher than the strike price of the option.

- **At-the-money (ATM):** An option is at-the-money if it has a zero intrinsic value, or if the current price of the underlying asset is equal to the strike price of the option.

To read and analyze option chains and quotes, you need to follow these steps:

- Select the underlying asset that you want to trade options on, such as a stock, an index, a commodity, a currency, or any other tradable security.

- Access the option chain for the underlying asset, using your trading platform, broker, or other sources, such as websites or apps.

- Choose the expiration date that matches your time horizon, and view the available strike prices and option types for that expiration date.

- Compare the bid and ask prices, the bid-ask spread, the last price, the volume, and the open interest of the options, and identify the options that have the best liquidity and demand.

- Compare the intrinsic and extrinsic value, the moneyness, and the implied volatility of the options, and identify the options that have the best value and potential.

- Choose the option or options that suit your trading objectives, strategies, and risk-reward trade-off, and execute your trade, using your trading platform, broker, or other sources.

How to use technical and fundamental analysis for options trading

Technical and fundamental analysis are two methods of analyzing the market and the underlying asset, and they can help you with your options trading decisions and actions. Technical analysis is the study of the price and volume patterns, trends, and indicators of the market and the underlying asset, using charts, tools, and techniques. Fundamental analysis is the study of the intrinsic value, quality, and performance of the market and the underlying asset, using financial statements, reports, and metrics.

To use technical and fundamental analysis for options trading, you need to follow these steps:

- Select the underlying asset that you want to trade options on, such as a stock, an index, a commodity, a currency, or any other tradable security.

- Access the technical and fundamental data and information for the underlying asset, using your trading platform, broker, or other sources, such as websites or apps.

- Perform technical analysis on the underlying asset, using charts, tools, and techniques, such as trend lines, support and resistance levels, moving averages, oscillators, indicators, patterns, etc. Technical analysis can help you to identify the direction, strength, and duration of the price movement of the underlying asset, and to determine the optimal entry and exit points for your options trades.

- Perform fundamental analysis on the underlying asset, using financial statements, reports, and metrics, such as earnings, revenue, growth, profitability, valuation, dividends, etc. Fundamental analysis can help you to assess the intrinsic value, quality, and performance of the underlying asset, and to determine the fair and expected price of the underlying asset.

- Combine technical and fundamental analysis on the underlying asset, and form a directional bias, a volatility outlook, a risk-reward trade-off, and a trading objective for your options trades. For example, if the technical analysis shows a bullish trend and a high volatility of the underlying asset, and the fundamental analysis shows a strong earnings and growth of the underlying asset, you may form a bullish and volatile bias, a high risk-high reward trade-off, and a market speculation objective for your options trades.

- Choose the option or options that match your directional bias, volatility outlook, risk-reward trade-off, and trading objective, and execute your trade, using your trading platform, broker, or other sources.

How to use indicators and signals for options trading

Indicators and signals are tools and techniques that help you to identify and confirm the price and volatility patterns, trends, and signals of the market and the underlying asset, and to generate trading ideas and signals for your options trades. Indicators and signals can be based on technical analysis, fundamental analysis, or a combination of both.

Some examples of indicators and signals for options trading are:

- **Technical indicators:** Technical indicators are mathematical calculations that are applied to the price and volume data of the underlying asset, and that produce graphical or numerical outputs that can be used to analyze the price and volatility patterns, trends, and signals of the underlying asset. Technical indicators can be classified into two types: trend-following indicators and oscillators. Trend-following indicators are indicators that follow the direction and strength of the price trend of the underlying asset, such as moving averages, trend lines, MACD, etc. Oscillators are indicators that measure the momentum and the overbought or oversold conditions of the price of the underlying asset, such as RSI, Stochastic, CCI, etc. Technical indicators can help you to identify the entry and exit points, the support and resistance levels, the trend reversals and continuations, and the trading signals for your options trades.

- **Fundamental indicators:** Fundamental indicators are financial ratios and metrics that are derived from the financial statements, reports, and data of the underlying asset, and that measure the intrinsic value, quality, and performance of the underlying asset. Fundamental indicators can be classified into four categories: profitability, growth, valuation, and dividend. Profitability indicators are indicators that measure the ability of the underlying asset to generate income and profit, such as earnings per share, return on equity, profit margin, etc. Growth indicators are indicators that measure the rate and the potential of the underlying asset to increase its income and profit, such as revenue growth, earnings growth, EPS growth, etc. Valuation indicators are indicators that measure the relative worth of the underlying asset, compared to its peers or the market, such as price-to-earnings ratio, price-to-book ratio, price-to-sales ratio, etc. Dividend indicators are indicators that measure the amount and the frequency of the dividends paid by the underlying asset, such as dividend yield, dividend payout ratio, dividend growth rate, etc. Fundamental indicators can help you to assess the fair and expected price, the quality and performance, and the trading signals for your options trades.

- **Combined indicators:** Combined indicators are indicators that combine technical and fundamental indicators, or multiple technical or fundamental indicators, to produce a more comprehensive and reliable analysis and signal for the underlying asset. Combined indicators can be created by using mathematical formulas, algorithms, or models, such as the Black-Scholes model, the binomial model, the Monte Carlo simulation, etc. Combined indicators can help you to enhance the accuracy and the efficiency of your options trading analysis and signals.

How to manage risk and reward in options trading

Risk and reward are two inseparable aspects of options trading, and they can have a significant impact on your options trading performance and results. Risk and reward can be measured by the breakeven point, the maximum profit, the maximum loss, and the probability of profit of an options strategy. Risk and reward can be managed by using various methods and techniques, such as position sizing, stop-loss, take-profit, hedging, diversification, etc.

Some examples of how to manage risk and reward in options trading are:

- **Position sizing:** Position sizing is the method of determining the optimal number of option contracts to trade, based on your trading capital, risk tolerance, and trading objectives. Position sizing can help you to control your risk exposure, to optimize your profit potential, and to avoid overtrading or undertrading. Position sizing can be calculated by using various formulas, such as the fixed percentage method, the fixed dollar method, the Kelly criterion, etc.

- **Stop-loss:** Stop-loss is the technique of setting a predetermined price or level at which you will close your option position, if the price of the underlying asset moves against your favor, to limit your loss. Stop-loss can help you to protect your trading capital, to reduce your emotional stress, and to prevent further losses. Stop-loss can be set by using various methods, such as the percentage method, the dollar method, the volatility method, etc.

- **Take-profit:** Take-profit is the technique of setting a predetermined price or level at which you will close your option position, if the price of the underlying asset moves in your favor, to lock in your profit. Take-profit can help you to secure your trading income, to reduce your opportunity cost, and to prevent profit reversal. Take-profit can be set by using various methods, such as the percentage method, the dollar method, the volatility method, etc.

- **Hedging:** Hedging is the technique of opening another option position or a position in another security or instrument, that has a negative or inverse correlation with your original option position, to reduce or eliminate the risk of your original option position. Hedging can help you to protect your original option position from adverse price movements, to increase your probability of profit, and to create a risk-free or arbitrage opportunity. Hedging can be done by using various methods, such as buying or selling the underlying asset, buying or selling another option, buying or selling a futures or a forward contract, etc.

- **Diversification:** Diversification is the technique of opening multiple option positions or positions in multiple securities or instruments, that have a low or no correlation with each other, to reduce the overall risk of your portfolio. Diversification can help you to reduce your portfolio volatility, to increase your portfolio return, and to create a balanced and efficient portfolio. Diversification can be done by using various methods, such as trading options on different underlying assets, trading options with different strike prices, expiration dates, or types of options, trading options with different strategies, etc.

In this chapter, we discussed the different types of options techniques and how to use them. We discussed the essential tools and skills for options trading, such as the trading platform and tools, the broker and account, the options education and resources, and the options trading plan and journal. We discussed how to read and analyze option chains and quotes, using the bid and ask prices, the bid-ask spread, the last price, the volume, the open interest, and the moneyness. We've discussed how to use technical and fundamental analysis for options trading, using charts, indicators, signals, financial statements, reports, and metrics. We also discussed how to use indicators and signals for options trading, using trend-following indicators, oscillators, and combined indicators.

SECTION 4

Options Trading Tips

In this chapter, you will learn some of the best practices and habits for successful options trading, some of the common mistakes and pitfalls to avoid in options trading, how to develop a trading plan and a trading journal, how to diversify and optimize your options portfolio, and how to leverage the power of compounding in options trading. These are the practical tips that you need to follow to trade options effectively and profitably.

The best practices and habits for successful options trading

Options trading can be rewarding, but also challenging, as it involves a high level of skill, knowledge, discipline, and risk management. To succeed in options trading, you need to adopt some of the best practices and habits that can help you to improve your trading performance and results. Some of the best practices and habits for successful options trading are:

- **Educate yourself:** Options trading requires a solid understanding of the options market, the options strategies, the options techniques, and the options risks. You need to educate yourself on the options basics, the options terminology, the options mechanics, and the options concepts, before you start trading options. You also need to keep learning and updating your options knowledge, as the options market is dynamic and evolving. You can use various options education and resources, such as books, courses, webinars, podcasts, blogs, forums, newsletters, etc., to learn and improve your options trading skills and strategies.

- **Practice and test:** Options trading requires a lot of practice and testing, as it involves a lot of trial and error, experimentation, and evaluation. You need to practice and test your options trading skills and strategies, before you trade with real money. You can use various options trading tools and platforms, such as simulators, demo accounts, paper trading, backtesting, etc., to practice and test your options trading ideas and signals, without risking your trading capital. You also need to review and analyze your options trading performance and results, and learn from your successes and failures, to improve your options trading skills and strategies.

- **Plan and execute:** Options trading requires a clear and consistent plan and execution, as it involves a lot of decision making and action taking. You need to plan and execute your options trading objectives, strategies, rules, and performance indicators, before you enter and exit your options trades. You can use various options trading techniques and methods, such as technical and fundamental analysis, indicators and signals, risk and reward management, position sizing, stop-loss, take-profit, hedging, diversification, etc., to plan and execute your options trades. You also need to follow and stick to your options trading plan and execution, and avoid any emotional or impulsive trading, to achieve your options trading objectives and goals.

- **Review and adjust:** Options trading requires a regular and systematic review and adjustment, as it involves a lot of feedback and adaptation. You need to review and adjust your options trading performance and results, and compare them with your options trading objectives and goals, after you exit your options trades. You can use various options trading tools and platforms, such as charts, indicators, scanners, calculators, etc., to review and adjust your options trading performance and results. You also need to identify and correct any errors or mistakes, and optimize any strengths or opportunities, in your options trading performance and results, to improve your options trading skills and strategies.

The common mistakes and pitfalls to avoid in options trading

Options trading can be risky, but also costly, as it involves a lot of potential errors or mistakes, and challenges or pitfalls. To avoid or minimize the negative impact of these errors or mistakes, and challenges or pitfalls, on your options trading performance and results, you need to be aware of and avoid some of the common mistakes and pitfalls in options trading. Some of the common mistakes and pitfalls to avoid in options trading are:

- **Trading without education:** Trading options without a proper education is one of the biggest and most common mistakes in options trading, as it can lead to a lot of confusion, frustration, and losses. Options trading is not a simple or easy activity, and it requires a solid understanding of the options market, the options strategies, the options techniques, and the options risks. Trading options without education can result in a lack of direction, strategy, and skill, and a high level of risk and uncertainty, in your options trading. To avoid this mistake, you need to educate yourself on the options basics, the options terminology, the options mechanics, and the options concepts, before you start trading options. You also need to keep learning and updating your options knowledge, as the options market is dynamic and evolving.

- **Trading without practice:** Trading options without practice is another big and common mistake in options trading, as it can lead to a lot of errors, failures, and losses. Options trading is not a theoretical or hypothetical activity, and it requires a lot of practice and testing, to develop and refine your options trading skills and strategies. Trading options without practice can result in a lack of experience, confidence, and performance, and a high level of risk and cost, in your options trading. To avoid this mistake, you need to practice and test your options trading skills and strategies, before you trade with real money. You can use various options trading tools and platforms, such as simulators, demo accounts, paper trading, backtesting, etc., to practice and test your options trading ideas and signals, without risking your trading capital.

- **Trading without a plan:** Trading options without a plan is another big and common mistake in options trading, as it can lead to a lot of indecision, inconsistency, and losses. Options trading is not a random or spontaneous activity, and it requires a clear and consistent plan and execution, to achieve your options trading objectives and goals. Trading options without a plan can result in a lack of purpose, direction, and criteria, and a high level of risk and emotion, in your options trading. To avoid this mistake, you need to plan and execute your options trading objectives, strategies, rules, and performance indicators, before you enter and exit your options trades.

You also need to follow and stick to your options trading plan and execution, and avoid any emotional or impulsive trading.

- **Trading without a review:** Trading options without a review is another big and common mistake in options trading, as it can lead to a lot of ignorance, complacency, and losses. Options trading is not a one-time or isolated activity, and it requires a regular and systematic review and adjustment, to improve your options trading skills and strategies. Trading options without a review can result in a lack of feedback, analysis, and learning, and a high level of risk and error, in your options trading. To avoid this mistake, you need to review and adjust your options trading performance and results, and compare them with your options trading objectives and goals, after you exit your options trades. You also need to identify and correct any errors or mistakes, and optimize any strengths or opportunities, in your options trading performance and results.

How to develop a trading plan and a trading journal

A trading plan and a trading journal are two essential tools that can help you to improve your options trading performance and results. A trading plan is a document that outlines your options trading objectives, strategies, rules, and performance indicators. A trading plan helps you to define your trading purpose, direction, and criteria, and to follow them consistently and systematically. A trading journal is a record of your options trading activities, results, and reflections. A trading journal helps you to track your trading performance, analyze your trading strengths and weaknesses, and improve your trading skills and strategies.

To develop a trading plan and a trading journal, you need to follow these steps:

- **Define your options trading objectives:** Your options trading objectives are the specific and measurable outcomes that you want to achieve from your options trading, such as income generation, risk hedging, market speculation, or wealth creation. Your options trading objectives should be realistic, attainable, and time-bound, and they should reflect your trading style, frequency, and capital. For example, your options trading objective could be to generate a monthly income of $1,000 from selling covered calls, with a trading capital of $10,000, and a trading frequency of once a week.

- **Choose your options trading strategies:** Your options trading strategies are the methods and techniques that you use to achieve your options trading objectives, such as buying or selling options, or combining multiple options, with different underlying assets, strike prices, expiration dates, or types of options. Your options trading strategies should be suitable, effective, and versatile, and they should match your directional bias, volatility outlook, risk-reward trade-off, and trading objectives. For example, your options trading strategy could be to sell a call option on XYZ stock, with a strike price above the current price of the stock, and an expiration date of one month, to generate income from the premium received, and to retain the upside potential of the stock.

- **Set your options trading rules:** Your options trading rules are the guidelines and criteria that you follow to enter and exit your options trades, such as the entry and exit signals, the position sizing, the stop-loss, the take-profit, the hedging, the diversification, etc. Your options trading rules should be clear, consistent, and rational, and they should help you to optimize your profit potential, and to minimize your risk exposure. For example, your options trading rule could be to enter a trade when the price of the underlying asset crosses above the 50-day moving average, and to exit a trade when the price of the underlying asset crosses below the 50-day moving average, or when the option expires, or when the option is exercised by the buyer.

- **Measure your options trading performance indicators:** Your options trading performance indicators are the metrics and statistics that you use to evaluate and monitor your options trading performance and results, such as the profit and loss, the return on investment, the win rate, the risk-reward ratio, the drawdown, the Sharpe ratio, etc. Your options trading performance indicators should be accurate, relevant, and consistent, and they should help you to assess your trading efficiency, effectiveness, and profitability. For example, your options trading performance indicator could be the return on investment, which is the percentage of the profit or loss divided by the initial investment, and which measures the return or the loss of your options trading relative to your trading capital.

- **Record your options trading activities, results, and reflections:** Your options trading activities, results, and reflections are the details and descriptions of your options trading actions, outcomes, and thoughts, that you write down in your trading journal. Your options trading activities, results, and reflections should be honest, comprehensive, and timely, and they should help you to track your trading performance, analyze your trading strengths and weaknesses, and improve your trading skills and strategies. For example, your options trading activity could be to sell a call option on XYZ stock, with a strike price of $60 and an expiration date of one month, and your options trading result could be to close the option position with a profit of $100, and your options trading reflection could be to review the reasons for your trading decision, the factors that affected your trading result, and the lessons that you learned from your trading experience.

How to diversify and optimize your options portfolio

An options portfolio is the collection of option positions that you hold, with different underlying assets, strike prices, expiration dates, or types of options. An options portfolio can help you to achieve your options trading objectives and goals, such as income generation, risk hedging, market speculation, or wealth creation. To diversify and optimize your options portfolio, you need to follow these steps:

- **Diversify your options portfolio:** Diversifying your options portfolio is the technique of opening multiple option positions or positions in multiple securities or instruments, that have a low or no correlation with each other, to reduce the overall risk of your portfolio. Diversifying your options portfolio can help you to reduce your portfolio volatility, to increase your portfolio return, and to create a balanced and efficient portfolio. Diversifying your options portfolio can be done by using various methods, such as trading options on different underlying assets, trading options with different strike prices, expiration dates, or types of options, trading options with different strategies, etc.

- **Optimize your options portfolio:** Optimizing your options portfolio is the technique of adjusting and modifying your option positions or positions in other securities or instruments, to improve the performance and the results of your portfolio. Optimizing your options portfolio can help you to enhance your portfolio efficiency, effectiveness, and profitability. Optimizing your options portfolio can be done by using various methods, such as closing, rolling, or adding to your option positions, hedging, diversifying, or rebalancing your portfolio, etc.

How to leverage the power of compounding in options trading

Compounding is the process of reinvesting your profits or returns from your options trading, to generate more profits or returns, and to increase your trading capital. Compounding is also known as the snowball effect, as it can help you to grow your trading capital exponentially over time. Compounding can help you to achieve your options trading objectives and goals, such as income generation, risk hedging, market speculation, or wealth creation. To leverage the power of compounding in options trading, you need to follow these steps:

- **Set a realistic and attainable compounding goal:** Your compounding goal is the specific and measurable outcome that you want to achieve from your options trading, by using the power of compounding, such as a target amount, a target return, or a target time. Your compounding goal should be realistic, attainable, and time-bound, and it should reflect your trading style, frequency, and capital. For example, your compounding goal could be to grow your trading capital from $10,000 to $100,000, by achieving a monthly return of 10%, in one year.

- **Choose a suitable and effective compounding strategy:** Your compounding strategy is the method and technique that you use to achieve your compounding goal, by reinvesting your profits or returns from your options trading, to generate more profits or returns, and to increase your trading capital. Your compounding strategy should be suitable, effective, and versatile, and it should match your directional bias, volatility outlook, risk-reward trade-off, and trading objectives. For example, your compounding strategy could be to sell covered calls on the underlying assets that you own, and to reinvest the premium received from selling the calls, to buy more underlying assets, and to repeat the process every month, until you reach your compounding goal.

- **Execute and monitor your compounding strategy:** Executing and monitoring your compounding strategy is the action and the evaluation that you do to implement and to track your compounding strategy, and to measure your progress and your results, towards your compounding goal. Executing and monitoring your compounding strategy should be clear, consistent, and rational, and they should help you to optimize your profit potential, and to minimize your risk exposure. For example, executing your compounding strategy could be to sell a call option on XYZ stock, with a strike price above the current price of the stock, and an expiration date of one month, and to collect the premium from selling the call option, and to buy more XYZ stock, and to repeat the process every month, until you reach your compounding goal. Monitoring your compounding strategy could be to measure your monthly return, your trading capital, and your compounding goal, and to compare them with your initial assumptions and expectations, and to adjust your compounding strategy, if necessary.

In this chapter, you learned some of the best practices and habits for successful options trading, some of the common mistakes and pitfalls to avoid in options trading, how to develop a trading plan and a trading journal, how to diversify and optimize your options portfolio, and how to leverage the power of compounding in options trading. You learned how to educate yourself, practice and test, plan and execute, and review and adjust your options trading skills and strategies. You learned how to avoid trading without education, practice, plan, or review, and how to correct any errors or mistakes, and optimize any strengths or opportunities, in your options trading performance and results. You also learned how to diversify your options portfolio, using different underlying assets, strike prices, expiration dates, or types of options, and how to optimize your options portfolio, using closing, rolling, or adding to your option positions, hedging, diversifying, or rebalancing your portfolio.

Conclusion

In this book, you have learned the basics, the strategies, the techniques, and the tips of options trading. You have learned what options are, how they work, why they are useful, and how to trade them. You have learned the different types of options, the different types of options strategies, the different types of options techniques, and the different types of options tips. You have learned how to use options to generate income, hedge risk, speculate on the market, or create wealth. You have learned how to use options to diversify and optimize your portfolio, and to leverage the power of compounding. You have learned how to use options to achieve your trading objectives and goals, and to improve your trading performance and results.

Options trading is a rewarding, but also challenging, activity that requires a high level of skill, knowledge, discipline, and risk management. To succeed in options trading, you need to adopt some of the best practices and habits, and to avoid some of the common mistakes and pitfalls that we have discussed in this book. You also need to keep learning and updating your options knowledge, as the options market is dynamic and evolving. You also need to keep practicing and testing your options skills and strategies, as options trading is not a theoretical or hypothetical activity, but a practical and real one.

We hope that this book has provided you with a solid foundation and a valuable guide for your options trading journey. We hope that this book has inspired you and motivated you to start or improve your options trading journey. We hope that this book has helped you to achieve your options trading objectives and goals, and to improve your options trading performance and results.

However, this book is not the end, but the beginning, of your options trading journey. There is much more to learn and explore in the options market, and there is always room for improvement and growth in your options trading skills and strategies. Therefore, we encourage you to continue your options trading education and practice, and to seek more options trading resources and references, for further learning and improvement.

Here are some of the additional resources and references that we recommend for further learning and improvement:

- Options as a Strategic Investment by Lawrence G. McMillan: This is one of the most comprehensive and authoritative books on options trading, covering the theory and the practice of options trading, with hundreds of examples and illustrations, and dozens of options strategies and techniques.

- **The Options Playbook by Brian Overby:** This is one of the most user-friendly and practical books on options trading, covering the basics and the strategies of options trading, with simple and clear explanations, and easy-to-follow diagrams and tables.

- **Option Volatility and Pricing by Sheldon Natenberg:** This is one of the most advanced and technical books on options trading, covering the concepts and the models of options pricing and volatility, with detailed and rigorous analysis and calculations, and complex and sophisticated options strategies and techniques.

- **Options Trading for Beginners by David Reese:** This is one of the most beginner-friendly and accessible books on options trading, covering the fundamentals and the essentials of options trading, with step-by-step and straightforward instructions, and helpful and realistic tips and examples.

- **The Options Institute:** This is the official educational arm of the Chicago Board Options Exchange (CBOE), the largest and the most popular options exchange in the world. The Options Institute offers a variety of online and offline courses, webinars, podcasts, blogs, newsletters, etc., for options traders of all levels and backgrounds.

- **Investopedia:** This is one of the most popular and reliable online sources of financial information and education, covering a wide range of topics and concepts, such as options, stocks, forex, commodities, etc. Investopedia offers a wealth of articles, videos, tutorials, quizzes, simulators, calculators, etc., for options traders of all levels and backgrounds.

- **Option Alpha:** This is one of the most innovative and interactive online platforms for options trading education and practice, offering a comprehensive and integrated system of courses, tools, podcasts, blogs, newsletters, etc., for options traders of all levels and backgrounds. Option Alpha also offers a unique and powerful feature called the Trade Optimizer, which helps options traders to find, analyze, and optimize their options trades, using artificial intelligence and machine learning.

Acknowledgement

I would like to express my sincere gratitude and appreciation to all the people who have contributed to the creation and completion of this book. Without their support and guidance, this book would not have been possible.

First and foremost, I would also like to thank my family, friends, and colleagues, for their constant love, support, and inspiration. They have been my motivation and my strength, and they have shared with me their insights and experiences in options trading.

I would like to thank Bing, who assisted me in the creation of my book. Bing was a reliable, helpful, and friendly source of information and inspiration.

Last but not least, I would like to thank you, the reader, for choosing this book, and for joining me on this options trading journey. I hope that this book will provide you with a solid foundation and a valuable guide for your options trading journey. I hope that this book will help you to achieve your options trading objectives and goals, and to improve your options trading performance and results.

I hope you found my service helpful and valuable. I would love to hear your honest feedback and ratings, as they will help me improve my service quality and customer satisfaction. Please let me know if you have any suggestions or comments on how I can serve you better.

Thank you for reading this book, and I wish you all the best in your options trading journey.